What on Earth is happening?

As I write this booklet, we all find ourselves in difficult times. For most of us life came to a virtual standstill at the beginning of 2020 due to the Coronavirus outbreak; a serious respiratory virus which quickly spread and became a pandemic. This meant that our Government had to impose many restrictions on our daily lives, in order to try and stop the spread of the virus in this country.

One year on we have been 'locked down' for the third time since Coronavirus began. Although the infection rates and number of deaths are now slowly reducing, we are still facing an unknown period of time where we have to be cautious because of this deadly virus; and it all seems very surreal.

Many folks are frightened and worried by what is happening and have asked for prayer, as they have found it difficult to cope and don't know where to turn for hope and comfort. Jobs have been lost because businesses of all kinds are being forced to close. People are anxious because money is tight and they have rents and mortgages to pay and families to feed.

> **Many folks are worried and have asked for prayer, as they have found it difficult to cope and don't know where to turn for hope and comfort**

At the time of writing (early 2021) 117,000 deaths have been recorded in the UK due to the virus. Unfortunately, most of the bereaved families were not able to be with their loved ones at the end of their lives to say 'goodbye', and this too has caused enormous stress and sadness.

There are many questions people have as to how and why this so suddenly came upon us. Just recently I received a telephone call from a lady who had been discussing the current events with another friend and wanted some answers. She asked me if I believe that the events we are currently seeing around the world, are 'from the Bible' as she put it. I told her that I do believe that what is happening is part of what the Bible says will happen in our world, in the days leading up to the 'Return of Jesus'.

For some years now, we have been seeing major things occurring more frequently in the world, in particular natural disasters; but also violence and hatred amongst the nations and individuals. This may all sound gloomy, but we only need to watch the news and read the papers to see how things really are! Our world is in crisis.

It seems that on every daily News report there are new and unexpected things happening, and this only adds to the fear and uncertainty folks feel about the future.

However, we need not despair! there is real hope, but it isn't going to be found in our scientists, doctors, governments, vaccines, or our own abilities to cope. It is found by putting our faith in God. Whatever else we choose to put our faith in, can let us down, but God will never let us down. All through the Bible, He reminds us of His promise that He will always be with us. In Isaiah chapter 41 and verse 10 it says this:

> Whatever else we choose to put our faith in, can let us down, but God will never let us down.

> *'Fear not, for I am with you; be not dismayed,*
> *for I am your God; I will strengthen you, I will help you,*
> *I will uphold you with my righteous right hand.'*

God never breaks His promises, so we can be encouraged in the middle of all the confusing and troubling things going on around us, because He knows precisely what is happening right now and is in control!

It may be that you are reading this booklet and have never heard about the fact that Jesus is going to come back to this Earth one day? You may have heard about Him; that He is the Son of God and came over two thousand years ago to live on earth and show men and women how God wants us to live; and that He loves and cares about us - but you may not know the whole story!

We all celebrate Christmas (when Jesus came as a baby into this world) and Easter (when He was crucified on a cross to take the punishment for our sins), but that isn't the end of the story of Jesus! God raised Him from the dead and He was taken back into heaven. He told His followers just before He went, that He would one day come back for those who truly believe in Him and are part of His family (the Church).

The Bible is also clear that this world as we know it, is not a permanent place. Sadly, when Adam and Eve (the first man and woman God created) disobeyed His instructions; things went bad in the world. Ever since then, they have become worse and we see today the results of men and women disregarding God's Commandments and rejecting His amazing love for us. God has told us, that this world as we know it will one day end, and a 'new heavens and a new earth' will be created for those who put their faith in Him.

> This world as we know it will one day end, and a 'new heavens and a new earth' will be created for those who put their faith in Him

The 'Return of Jesus' is something that is seldom preached about in many churches these days, yet in some church services, people collectively join in a response by saying *'Christ has died, Christ is risen, Christ will come again'!* Do we really believe that? The first two events in this statement have already happened and were witnessed by many people at the time, and were recorded in the Bible. The last also according to the Bible; could happen at any time and may be sooner than we think! So are we ready to meet Jesus?

We are not given the date or time when Jesus will come back, but we are given 'signs' in the Bible to watch out for when His return is getting near. Some of those signs are becoming evident today.

Many people will brush off the unusual events we see occurring in our world, as having 'happened all through history'; being 'normal'; 'are due to global warming or Climate change etc'. but no-one can deny the increasing frequency and intensity of what is happening today, particularly in the natural world. In the Bible, the book of 2 Timothy Chapter 3 and verses 1-5 also tells us how men and women will be in the 'last days' just before Jesus returns. It makes interesting reading and describes exactly the attitudes and thinking of folks today who have no regard for God.

> **Wonderful times are ahead for those who put their faith in God and believe what He has told us in the Bible!**

The Bible is our 'handbook for life', it's not fiction, fantasy or a figment of someone's imagination, it is a God-given book and is truly amazing. It is constantly being proven to be true in its contents and prophesies, and we can take great comfort and reassurance in these troubled days, that wonderful times are ahead for those who put their faith in God and believe what He has told us in the Bible!

Two verses from the Bible to remind us of God's love and care:

'For I know the plans I have for you' declares the Lord,
'plans to prosper you and not to harm you,

plans to give you hope and a future'

Jeremiah 29 verse 11 (NIV)

'… and surely I am with you always, to the very end of the age.'

Matthew 28 verse 20 (NIV)

Climate Change

For some years now we have been hearing about Global Warming and Climate Change, and many folks particularly young people, are concerned about the future of our planet and we are all being told in no uncertain terms that we must change our ways. In the past the earth has gone through some significant temperature and climate changes and although those changes were not thought to be the result of human activity, scientists have had a change of mind and now believe that human activity is the main cause, although there is much disagreement about the facts!

There is no doubt that major things are happening to our world, so we do need to think about the issue. As Christians, we should of course think and behave responsibly concerning damage caused to God's beautiful world through human activity, and there are things we can do to help reduce this, but we should not get caught up and concentrate our focus on 'environmentalism' - a political movement, and over which many folks are fanatical and which has become like a 'religion'.

When God created the world and everything in it, He gave us the responsibility of 'caretaking' the natural world and managing the resources we have wisely. We are to preserve and protect nature and the beauty around us.

We are to preserve and protect nature and beauty around us

God has given us all the resources we need to feed, clothe and house us all, and these resources are renewable and are replenished by natural means i.e. the sun and rain. Sadly, our beautiful earth is being denuded by our greed and desire for more and more 'things' and is suffering because of it.

In 2020 there was a programme on the television in which we were made aware of the problems we are facing in our world being caused by human behaviour and Climate change; in particular extinction, and the facts were alarming.

There has been a loss of Biodiversity (the variety of life on earth—plants, animals etc.) because the world is getting too warm and many birds and creatures cannot survive. Their habitats and food sources have changed due to deforestation—90% of forests around the world have already been lost. There are on average 100,000 trawlers at any one time, fishing and sweeping our seas. We are completely destroying the natural balance of fish across the world; the oceans are littered with plastic, and the waters are warming—to mention a few of the things covered in that programme, and we were left wondering what on earth we can do to change this, if anything!

I recently read an article which quoted a report by Oxfam stating that 'more than four times the number of natural disasters are occurring now than two decades ago.' We are also being warned that climate change will increase the frequency of extreme weather events such as floods, droughts, heatwaves, hurricanes and tornadoes - according to the report.

...an article quoted a report by Oxfam stating that 'more than four times the number of natural disasters are occurring now than two decades ago

Things in our world are becoming quite serious and many Christians believe that we are living in the times that Jesus spoke of in Matthew chapter 24 in the Bible. Many of these things we are experiencing now are exactly what the Bible says will be happening in the 'last days' before Jesus comes back to this earth.

There are ways in which we can and should care more about our world, but 'saving the planet' as many are saying we must, should not be our main focus, particularly if we are Christians. I recently read a thought-provoking quote 'Environmental issues are important, but they are not the most important issues facing mankind'. More important than anything else in life should be our relationship with God, who created us and sent Jesus to this earth to show us how to live as He intended us to.

The earth as we know it, our present home, will not last forever and God has made that clear in the Bible. He has told us that one day this earth will be destroyed and He will create a 'new heaven and a new earth' because this world has been spoiled by sin.

Climate change is real and may or may not be human-caused, but one thing is for certain; we need to focus less on our concerns about 'Mother Earth' - as some call our world - and more on God our Heavenly Father - whose world it is, and who is in total control of it. He has planned how long it will exist and be our home!

There are verses in the Bible that sum this up:

'The earth is the LORD's, and everything in it.
The world and all its people belong to him.
For he laid the earth's foundation on the seas
and built it on the ocean depths.

Who may climb the mountain of the LORD?
Who may stand in his holy place?
Only those whose hands and hearts are pure,
who do not worship idols
and never tell lies.
They will receive the LORD's blessing
and have a right relationship with God their Saviour'

(Psalm 24 verses 1– 5 (New Living Translation)

What we need to be doing right now as we see all these things happening around us which are damaging our planet, is turn back to God. We need to ask His forgiveness for the misuse of our beautiful natural world. We are all responsible in some way!

Since what the Bible says is coming true before our eyes, and our world is in trouble in many ways; we are told to be ready to meet Jesus when we see these things begin to happen! Are you ready?

We need to ask His forgiveness for the misuse of our beautiful natural world. We are all responsible in some way!

Coronavirus

We often hear folks say 'You never know what the future holds'. That saying became a stark reality in late January 2020. Coronavirus or Covid19 as it's also known, reached the United Kingdom.

This very unpleasant and dangerous virus affects the respiratory system, and in no time at all it became a pandemic. It first appeared in China and very quickly spread around the world. Many people became sick and the deaths rose daily. Our National Health Service was becoming overwhelmed by people needing hospital care, and emergency hospital facilities were set up in towns and cities around the country, as it rapidly spread.

By March, the Government had imposed a 'lockdown' which was to change our lives dramatically, and would curtail our much valued freedom. It was unbelievable how in what seemed like a matter of days, our lives had been turned upside down. People rushed to the stores and in panic brought foods and supplies, as at the time we had no idea how long the 'lockdown' would last. We were all told we had to 'socially distance' from each other by staying at least 2 metres apart. We couldn't visit friends and family and our towns and cities became like 'ghost towns', with very few cars on the roads. Only essential services were open such as food stores, petrol stations and pharmacies. We couldn't go to the hairdresser or dentist; restaurants and most other hospitality places were closed. We were allowed to go out for exercise each day (keeping our distance from others), and to go and buy essentials.

Wherever we went there were queues and we were told what to do, it felt as though we were being 'herded' like animals. Of course, it was all in the interest of our own safety, but it seemed like an unpleasant dream. The 'lockdown' lasted for several months. The psychological effect on folks became concerning. The lack of leisure facilities; social contact; spiritual input by not being allowed to go to Church; family separation etc. all had a massive impact after the first few weeks, and fear and worry crept in as businesses were forced to close, unable to withstand the financial losses.

> Of course, it was all in the interest or our own safety, but it seemed like an unpleasant dream. The lockdown lasted for several months

In turn that led to loss of jobs and earnings; children were out of school for months. Holidays and travel had to be cancelled, causing much loss and hardship. What in the world was happening?

Eventually in the summer months, the case numbers and death rates dropped somewhat, and some of the restrictions were lifted and it seemed we might be beginning to get back to normal. However, in order to make sure the number of people infected was kept down, face masks were made mandatory in shops and other places. Social distancing and constant handwashing still had to be maintained, but the misery of having to walk around wearing a face mask felt as though we were 'gagged' and yet another freedom had been curtailed - the freedom to talk to each other.

Most people adjusted and conformed, but there were many who felt that the restrictions didn't apply to them

Most people adjusted and conformed, but there were many who felt the restrictions didn't apply to them and when public houses and restaurants were opened up again, the 'rules' went out of the window. Sadly, heavier restrictions had to be imposed because of the minority who chose to ignore advice; and a tier system was brought in so that rather than a nationwide 'lockdown', the areas worst affected by the transmission of the virus, were put in the highest tier and those not so bad were put in a less restrictive tier.

As the end of the year approached, University Students were confined to their houses of residence and much discussion ensued as to whether they would be allowed to go home for Christmas. Families and friends were permitted to form a 'bubble' with one other household and as Christmas 2020 got nearer the Government set rules that several households would be allowed to meet together for 5 days over the Christmas period. Unfortunately that had to be changed, as many folks still did not abide by the rules and the virus began to spread rapidly, so it ended up with families being able to meet on Christmas Day only and with a very limited number. It was miserable and like no other Christmas we'd known before.

After Chrismas a new variant of the virus appeared and a third 'lockdown' was imposed. At the time of writing there are plans to release the country of all restrictions (virus permitting!) by mid-June, almost 18 months after they were first imposed!

Once the virus had taken hold in 2020 Pharmaceutical companies had started working on a vaccine to combat it. This was happening in several countries and we now have several options of a vaccine and people are being vaccinated according to their need for urgent protection such as front line workers in hospitals and senior citizens of 80 and 90+, gradually they are vaccinating the whole population who are willing to take it.

The hope is that it will at least enable us to get back to some sort of normality, whatever that will be!

Some folks are hesitant about taking the vaccines as they have been produced very quickly and there is concern regarding the safety and brevity of testing. Others are unable to take it due to pre-existing health conditions. However most people are being encouraged to take it to protect themselves and others, as this virus doesn't seem to be going away any time soon. The hope is that it will at least enable us to get back to some sort of normality, whatever that will be! so we must obey the rules.

There is little of our lives and society which has been unaffected by this Pandemic - the loss of life, devastation of jobs and livelihoods, interruption of young peoples' schooling, huge damage to our economy to mention just some of the effects - but there has been an increase in mental health problems too, where folks have been isolated for long periods of time, especially in care homes, where families have been unable to visit.

…there will always be consequences to ignoring the rules, this applies in life both physically and spiritually

This has been a very sobering experience, and there are serious lessons for us all in this. We should stick to the rules—they are there for a reason—our wellbeing! Many folks have doubted them, disputed them and disobeyed them; but there are always consequences to ignoring rules, this applies in life both physically and spiritually.

When God created this beautiful world and us as the epitome of His creation; He also set rules in place for our good and to keep us safe. However, things went bad for mankind when the rules were broken by Adam and Eve's disobedience in the garden of Eden. Our world was spoiled, and today we are seeing the long-term consequences of that disobedience!

Although this all sounds really depressing—there is hope, and we can get through this tough time with God's help. You may be thinking, 'but I don't believe in God'; that may be so, but is there anyone else you know who can give you real peace of heart and mind, in the middle of all this? Anyone who can tell you assuredly that the future will be fine, and that you will have all you need, even when you can't see how you will manage for one more day?

In the book of Psalms in the Bible, there are many verses which tell us what to do when things are tough and threaten to overwhelm us, and there seems to be no real answer. Here are a few:

'Trust in Him at all times, O people;
Pour out your heart before Him;
God is a refuge for us.'

Psalm 62 verse 8

'The Lord is good,
A stronghold in the day of trouble,
And He knows those who take refuge in Him.'

Nahum 1 verse 7

'The righteous cry out, and the LORD hears them;
he delivers them from all their troubles.
The LORD is close to the broken-hearted
and saves those who are crushed in spirit.'

Psalm 34 verses 17-18

Our world is not in a very good place right now, and we need to ask for God's help and believe He will hear us when we pray to Him; but first we need to ask His forgiveness for our unbelief and wrongdoing; the Bible tells us that when we do that, God will listen to our prayers and answer them.

Our Country has gone far away from when it was considered a 'Christian' country, and when we look at the news and read the papers, we can see just how bad things have become. Another verse from the Bible which is appropriate for the days we are living in, is found in the book of Chronicles chapter 7 and verse 14 and it says this:

'If my people, which are called by my name,
shall humble themselves,
pray and seek my face and turn from their wicked ways,
then I will hear from heaven, and will forgive their sin,
and will heal their land.'

Although this was directed at the people of Israel when it was written, it applies to us today too. This doesn't mean that only Christian people should pray either, it means there is a worldwide need for folks to turn back to God!

Many millions of people around the world have turned to God and found peace of mind, help and comfort and forgiveness.

God loves us and is longing to help us. He wants us to turn to Him for help at this time and any other time that things get beyond us. He will not disappoint us. Many millions of people around the world have turned to God and found peace of mind, help and comfort and forgiveness. He has plans for every person He's created and He assures us they are good!

God wisely doesn't allow us to know the future, but He has told us He will be with us always, if we put our faith and trust in Him. Why would we not want to, when life is so uncertain?

'Oh taste and see that the Lord is good:
blessed is the man that trusts in Him'

Psalm 34 verse 8

Racism

All through history we read that there have been problems between people groups of differing cultures, lifestyles and skin colour. Sadly these issues still exist today and are the root of some awful things happening in our world. There is an answer of course, and it's found in the Bible, a book which has been sidelined and many disregard its relevance today. So let's go back in time and take a look at Racism from a Christian perspective.

All humans are descended from Adam and Eve, so all are related. From the Biblical perspective there is one biological race. This has been confirmed by scientific studies on the human genome. Biblically and scientifically therefore there is no defence of racism! In the book of Acts chapter 17 in the bible, it says this *'From one man He made every nation of men, that they should inhabit the whole earth; and He determined the times set for them and the exact places where they should live.'*

The question that many people ask is, if we all descended from Adam how come there are so many differences in people? By Genesis chapter 6, men had begun to increase on the earth, but sadly they also became very wicked, because everyone had inherited the sinful nature from Adam and Eve after they disobeyed God.

God was grieved and decided He would wipe mankind from the face of the earth. But one man found favour in God's eyes—Noah, who was a righteous man, and blameless among the people of his time, and he was Godly. We all know the story of Noah and the Ark, and how God preserved Noah and his family, who eventually re-populated the earth.

At that time the world had one language and common speech. As men began to move eastward and spread out, they found a pleasant place and started to build a city with a tower that would reach to the heavens, and they wanted to make a name for themselves and stay there. They rebelled against God and refused to spread out and populate the wider world as He had told them to. Because of this, God judged them and divided their language into many languages, and groups separated from each other and moved away.

As a consequence the people groups became genetically isolated by marrying and having children within their group, and as time passed formed their own cultures and ways of doing things. As a result certain features, such as skin shade became dominant in certain groups. Human skin is one colour—brown—but in many varying shades, due to a pigment called melanin which is in our skin.

In the evolutionary ideas—'races' descended from different ancestors, separated by location and time. In Biblical terms and history, we are all one race—the human race.

A person's skin colour should not incite prejudice or 'racist' comments. We are all equal before God!

In some cultures, folks are 'racially' programmed because of skin colour, and because of those roots; the way the world thinks and the evolutionary thinking; people are inclined to look on the outside of a person rather than the inside—the 'real' person that God sees. We need to think differently!

> In the evolutionary ideas – 'races' descended from different ancestors, separated by location and time. In Biblical terms and history, we are all one race – the human race

The account of the Tower of Babel in the Bible, where God divided the languages, is where we need to look to be able to understand how different languages, cultures and people groups began.

'Grace' rather than 'race' is the way for Christians particularly, to grow in their love for God and others. Unfortunately many Church

Leaders never tackle the subject of race relations because it's so divisive, but unity concerning cultural and ethnic matters should be taught, not because it's 'topical' but because it's the teaching in God's Word—to 'love one another'.

> Our thinking, teaching and living must be based on reconciliation and guided by our understanding of God's perspective in the Bible

When a person becomes a real Christian, they become part of God's family and there is no division. Our thinking, teaching and living must be based on reconciliation and guided by our understanding of God's perspective in the Bible.

The root problem of bad 'race' relations is sin, and the only solution is to remember that when Jesus died on the cross it was for every human being! The real issue is about 'sin' not 'skin'. This should put a completely different light on how we see our brothers and sisters from different countries and cultural backgrounds.

In 2020, an incident took place in Minneapolis in America which shook the world. A black man called George Floyd had been to a shop and allegedly paid for some cigarettes with a counterfeit $20 bill. He was subsequently arrested and what followed was horrific—he was murdered by a Police Officer in full view of bystanders. Some people had filmed the events on their mobile phones, and this quickly spread to the media and around the world. This immediately set off protests about the treatment of black people and an activist group which had been started in 2013 called 'Black Lives Matter, became involved. Sadly this outcry led to huge and destructive demonstrations around the world under the 'Racism' banner. Everywhere now we see the slogan BLM or Black Lives Matter - of course they do, but *every* life matters in God's eyes.

Sadly the world's history of slavery has also been brought once again to the fore. Slavery is mentioned in the Bible as being common in the Middle East as far back as ancient Egypt. It has even been said recently that the Bible condoned slavery, but this is not so. God listed slave traders among the 'worst of sinners' in 1 Timothy chapter 10. God's own people, the Israelites were taken as slaves by the Egyptians, who were severely punished by God after the Israelites were eventually released.

> It has been said recently that the Bible condoned slavery, but this is not so. God listed slave traders among 'the worst of sinners

Many people, all through history have worked under a 'master' or a 'boss', but in no way are they any less a precious person and must be regarded and treated as such, and with love and respect by everyone.

The Bible, our 'handbook' for life, clearly tells us how we should treat our fellow human beings irrespective of colour or culture. No one has the right to treat another as a 'lesser' person than themselves. God said so! I recently heard a quote which said 'We are all brown— simply in varying shades'!

'Racism' is a terrible issue in our world, and there are very many other examples of it, not the least anti-Semitism. The only answer is for us all to look at how God sees humankind—the epitome of His creation! He loves us all and desires that we should love each other—without prejudice or exception and remember that we are all made in God's image!

An interesting quote from Nelson Mandela:

'No one is born hating another person because of the colour of his skin, or his background, or his religion. People must learn to hate, and if they can learn to hate, they can be taught to love.'

Some years ago my Husband and I lived in East Africa, where we worked as Missionaries. We soon realised that there was much more the folks there could teach us, than we could teach them. Although poorer in material possessions, they were so much 'richer' in their kindness, their love for God, His Word, and each other; and their generosity toward us was overwhelming and we were treated as though we were family. 'Skin colour' didn't matter at all! We may have gone there to help them, but we came back changed people from our experiences! Perhaps we should adopt the same attitude towards folks coming to the UK from other countries!

The Media

The 'media' is the means by which masses of people are reached via Television, Radio, Newspapers and nowadays the Internet. The main aim of the media is to gather and communicate news and information as quickly as possible, and it's often presented in a dramatic and 'attention grabbing' way. It's amazing how sophisticated the means of spreading news has become, but is it a good thing? Of course many will say, we need it so that we can know what's going on in our world; others will say they don't engage with it very much as it's a mixed blessing and almost always depressing!

Whatever our opinions, it's here to stay and advances in communication are changing rapidly. The media has a huge impact on human life. It gives us information and knowledge we may not otherwise be able to access; it gives us warnings; it reveals details about peoples' lives; to mention just a few things, but there is a side to it that is not good. It can be judgemental, biased, distorting, and manipulative. There are massive amounts of money involved in maintaining it. It can ruin lives, and cause hurt and suffering to people it 'spotlights' such as royalty and celebrities.

Over the past year, many have become very fearful and worried about our world because of the way important news is presented, for example the Coronavirus pandemic; threats of war, attacks and retaliation from other countries in the form of terrorism. We have been subjected to horrific scenes of devastation and killing, which in reality we don't need to see. Sadly the media seems inclined to revel in the bad and minimise things which are good and encouraging. Of course there are many good things to report, but they seem to be relegated to the last minute or two of the news programmes, and put in the small print in the papers.

...there are good many good things to report, but they seem to be relegated to the last minute of two of the news programmes

So why is this? We are living in a 21st Century world which in the main has rejected God and much of what is good and right. Folks are eager to hear things which are sensational and sometimes damning about others. Sex and violence seem to be a 'must' inclusion in many television programmes and even our 'soaps' are now including things which not too many years ago would be 'banned' from the screen. What has happened? Unfortunately it seems to be all about money and giving people what the media think we want (or should be looking at) but is it really what folks want?

In 2012 our country was declared a 'secular' country and no longer 'Christian'. That was a sad day for our once respected nation. That being said, Christians know that such things as we are seeing now will be tolerated; but at a certain point, God will intervene in the affairs of humankind, and will sort out what is happening to His world, just as He did in the 'days of Noah', when people had turned away from Him and had become really wicked.

There is a source of information available to us which covers ethics; past, present and future events; warnings; sound advice; help, comfort and hope for the future - it is of course the Bible. If we spent even half as much time reading the Bible, as we spend reading the newspapers, watching TV and listening to the news, we would probably be less anxious, stressed or frightened about the future and what we see happening around us. There is a verse in the Bible which can change our thinking in the middle of all the troubles we see and hear about via the media. It's found in Philippians Chapter 4 verse 8 and says this:

'Whatever is true, whatever is noble, whatever is right, whatever is pure, whatever is lovely, whatever is admirable - if anything is excellent or praiseworthy - think about such things.'

I recently read an article which reminded us that we live in a world which is constantly bombarding us with messages, images and views that are not compatible with a biblical worldview. It's possible that even Christians can begin to think in secular rather than biblical ways if the popular culture begins to change their values. Thinking about the words in the verse from Philippians 4 is particularly appropriate when evaluating our own consumption of the media i.e. television programmes, movies, music, reading matter etc. This doesn't mean that everything we watch, listen to or read has to be overtly Christian, but what we take in should bring us closer to God, give us a greater desire to obey Him, and be prepared to share the 'good news' about Jesus!. If what we are taking in much of the time doesn't have this effect on our thinking then we are not taking notice of what we are advised in the Bible to do about our thoughts. If we were to take this verse seriously surely our media consumption habits would have to change. It's so easy to get caught up in it all and waste precious time. Makes you think doesn't it?

Social Media

This is a very emotive topic! There are many who consider it a brilliant thing and others who think its damaged our society. Of course there are very definitely two aspects to it. On the one hand it has 'connected' people in so many ways, on the other hand it has also isolated people.

During the recent difficult periods of being 'locked down' or isolated because of the current pandemic; social media without doubt, has been invaluable in bringing people together when we are prevented from meeting as families and friends in person, or in clubs, gyms, church, work etc. It's great for those who have it available to them, but not so good for those who don't. Many sections of our society have been able to keep going by using it to work from home and keep their businesses ticking over; Churches have used a platform called 'Zoom' (where two or more people can connect and see and hear each other) this enables folks to share in Church Services, and many have held family gatherings and other meetings via this, it has been a tremendous help and comfort in being able to see and talk to each other.

Unfortunately though there are still many who don't have the modern technology, particularly some elderly folks and those who don't have the money to buy it. They have felt very cut off and have been really badly affected by the long periods of isolation; and loneliness has been a serious mental health issue.

As amazing as it all is, many feel that social media also has a 'downside'. There have been issues concerning young people with bullying; also serious issues concerning how they see themselves. There is a condition called Body Dysmorphic Disorder (BDD) this is a mental health condition where a person spends a lot of time worrying about flaws in their appearance (flaws which are often unnoticed by other people). This condition can be made worse by so-called 'perfect looks and bodies' portrayed via the media. There have even been a number of suicides among young folk because of the pressures they are under from the internet and social media sites. Some sites have been used for pornography and 'grooming' of young children and teens, which has caused considerable damage and concern for parents. The other concern with social media sites is that they are used by people who are racially prejudiced, and many people, including footballers and celebrities have been badly abused online.

> As amazing as it all is, many feel that social media also has a 'downside'

This sort of thing begs the question 'How much are we doing as Christians who use social media, to counteract some of this content'?

Although I am not that proficient in using all the technology available today, I do find it invaluable in my Christian work and for communication purposes. Some folks seem to have all the technology that's going, but as it is constantly changing, it becomes harder to keep up with, and that in itself can be stressful, costly and puts pressure on folks!

> No matter how we travel around these days, be it in our cars, on trains, buses, planes, even ships – we can be in touch with people most of the time

The one piece of technology that has made a very noticeable difference in our society is the mobile phone! No matter how we travel around these days, be it in our cars, on trains, buses, planes, even ships—we can be in touch with people most of the time. It has certainly changed our communication skills. Very few people write letters these days, it's all done by text messages and Emails; there is a distinct lack of conversation between folks in restaurants, coffee shops, social gatherings, and whilst walking around the streets or in shops even; because everyone is either on their mobile phone checking their messages, calls, emails, or looking up things on the Internet. It has become quite an anti-social world and we are losing the art of face to face communication, which is really sad, and it's all in the name of progress??

So much of the current technology is also being used in our churches as well. There is nothing wrong with that of course, but I have to admit, many Bibles are gathering dust on the shelf having been replaced by smartphones and Ipads which are 'more convenient' to take to Church and Bible Studies etc. I have those bits of technology, but somehow there is nothing like using my Bible in Church or when I am speaking. Call me old-fashioned, but there is something so precious about my Bible with all its handwritten notes and markings which mean something; that I couldn't honestly substitute it with modern technology, unless I had no choice!

Technology and the media is all about communication, but there is absolutely no substitute for communication with God – Prayer! We can sometimes get so caught up with everything that is available to us, that we have less time to spend in talking to God! It's all too easy to even skip a daily quiet-time, to rush and check emails and text messages, or watch a favourite programme on TV.

All we have in this world to make life easier is fine, but one day we will all stand before God with nothing in our hands. Will we be embarrassed by the huge amount of precious time He gave us whilst here on earth, which was wasted and consumed by the 'media' in all its forms? Psalm 90 verse 12 says:

'Teach us to number our days and recognize how few they are; help us to spend them as we should.' (Living Bible)

Homelessness

One of the saddest things to witness in our generally wealthy society today is the problem of homelessness. Day after day we see folks young and old sleeping rough on our streets in shop doorways, under bridges and in makeshift camps, as they have no home to go to.

There are many and varied reasons why people end up living rough; and most of us can't begin to imagine what it must be really like to have no warm bed at night, no cupboard with food in, no family and friends around to love and care for us, no money even to buy a few necessities and having to rely on the generosity of others to provide food.

Often people are critical of folks having to live this way, accusing them of being lazy, addicts, a blight on society and other unkind

> **Often people are critical of folks having to live this way... without even knowing who they are or why they find themselves in this position**

remarks, without even knowing who they are or why they find themselves in that position. There is a sad story behind every person who is homeless.

The main cause of homelessness today, according to charities, is welfare reform, which has meant that more people are losing their homes because they are unable to pay rents which have become very expensive. There have also been many job losses due to the pandemic, particularly in the lower paid sector such as hospitality. People have been struggling to make ends meet and have found themselves in difficulty and unable to cope.

Homelessness can also be due to family and relationship breakdown, and this has been made worse recently by the Coronavirus pandemic; where families have been 'locked down' together for long periods and that has probably caused more relationship issues.

I asked one Charity what we can all do to help. There were several answers. The public needs to be more sympathetic towards the homeless folk, as their situation is not necessarily their own fault or choice; as many people think! One other thing that homeless people living on the streets need, is for folks to speak to them, even if it's only a 'hello' or maybe just a smile. The point was also made, that we have no idea whether a simple gesture like that maybe the last time anyone speaks to them, in case they don't make it! That really was a sobering thought, and we need to pray regularly for homeless folk, as they are vulnerable in all kinds of ways.

Some years ago, I had an experience which left an indelible mark on my heart.

I went to visit my sister in Cardiff one weekend to do some Christmas shopping together. We had finished our day's shopping and were on our way back to the station for me to catch my train home. We came out of one of the large stores behind which was an alleyway. There were quite a few folk walking along it loaded down with shopping bags. We had gone a few yards and noticed a young lad sitting on the ground wrapped in a blanket. He looked very pale and tired.

> ...he had come to the UK to a job, but had recently been made redundant, and because of that, had lost his accommodation also.

We stopped and my Sister asked if he was ok and would he like something to eat or drink. We noticed he had an accent, so asked him where he was from, but he wouldn't say. We asked how he had become homeless and he told us that he had come to the UK to a job, but had recently been made redundant, and because of that, had lost his accommodation also. We asked why he wouldn't tell us where he was from. He told us that the day before a lady had given him some money to help him and asked where he had come from. He told her Poland. Immediately she turned on him and said 'If I'd known that, I wouldn't have given you anything', and she'd made him cry.

We were shocked and saddened and tried to comfort him. We were able to direct him to a shelter my Sister knew of, where he could get some food and a bed for the night.

How often have we walked past someone sitting alone on the street, clearly without all the things we have and take for granted? That experience changed my thinking and I am reminded of the fact the Jesus too was 'homeless' during His ministry here on earth. He relied on friends and the kindness of others to feed and support Him. We know this because in Matthew chapter 8 and verse 20, He said 'Foxes have holes and birds of the air have nests, but the Son of Man has no place to lay his head'.

We all have the responsibility of caring for those less fortunate than ourselves.

Jesus understands the situation of homeless people and provides help and support for them through those who care. We shouldn't just leave that job to the 'charities'. We all have the responsibility of caring for those less fortunate than ourselves. God sees our hearts and reminds us in the Bible that one day we will all stand before Him and be judged by what we have done or neglected to do to help the needy. In Matthew 25 verses 44-45 Jesus said:

> 'Truly I tell you, whatever you did for one of the least of these brothers and sisters of mine, you did for me'

In a country such as ours, where we have so much, it's incomprehensible that there are so many folks living lonely and sad lives on our streets. We spend so much time, effort and money on things that are not important, while precious human beings are suffering in this way.

There is a saying which we would do well to remember and that is:

'There, but for the Grace of God, go I'

'No eye has seen,
no ear has heard,
no mind has conceived
what God has
prepared for those
who love him.'

1 Corinthians 2:9